THE 10™

Most Essential Natural Resources

Deneena Davis

Series Editor
Jeffrey D. Wilhelm

D1376669

Much thought, debate, and research went into choosing and ranking the 10 items in each book in this series. We realize that everyone has his or her own opinion of what is most significant, revolutionary, amazing, deadly, and so on. As you read, you may agree with our choices, or you may be surprised — and that's the way it should be!

Franklin Watts

an imprint of

SCHOLASTIC

www.scholastic.com/librarypublishing

A Rubicon book published in association with Scholastic Inc.

Rubicon © 2008 Rubicon Publishing Inc.
www.rubiconpublishing.com

Associate Publishers: Kim Koh, Miriam Bardswich
Project Editor: Amy Land
Editor: Joyce Thian
Creative Director: Jennifer Drew
Project Manager/Designer: Jeanette MacLean
Graphic Designer: Andrea Jankun

The publisher gratefully acknowledges the following for permission to reprint copyrighted material in this book.

Every reasonable effort has been made to trace the owners of copyrighted material and to make due acknowledgment. Any errors or omissions drawn to our attention will be gladly rectified in future editions.

"Diamond miners cruelly exploited" (excerpt) by Michelle Glavic. From *Toronto Star*, February 14, 2007. Reprinted with permission.

Cover image: Oil Pumping Units at Sunset–© Lowell Georgia/Corbis

Library and Archives Canada Cataloguing in Publication

Davis, Deneena
    The 10 most essential natural resources / Deneena Davis.

Includes index.
ISBN: 978-1-55448-549-9

    1. Readers (Elementary). 2. Readers—Natural resources.
I. Title. II. Title: Ten most essential natural resources.

PE1117.D38 2007   428.6   C2007-906853-7

1 2 3 4 5 6 7 8 9 10   10   17 16 15 14 13 12 11 10 09 08

Printed in Singapore

Contents

Introduction: Ecological Gems 4

Gold 6
This precious metal has some uses that might surprise you.

Diamonds 10
What are people willing to do to get these sparkling gems?

Natural Gas 14
Powering modern society into the 21st century and beyond …

Coal 18
Burning this rock has given humankind a source of energy for thousands of years, but some say it's time to stop.

Oil 22
Why might the world's reliance on this fossil fuel have many experts concerned for our future?

Iron 26
One of the most revolutionary resources in human history.

Salt 30
Any geographer worth his or her salt would agree that this mineral is essential!

Trees 34
Though trees are considered renewable, they still need to be carefully managed for the benefit of all living things on the planet.

Soil 38
There is no such thing as plain old dirt …

Freshwater 42
Could we be running out of this precious resource?

We Thought … 46

What Do You Think? 47

Index 48

6

18

34

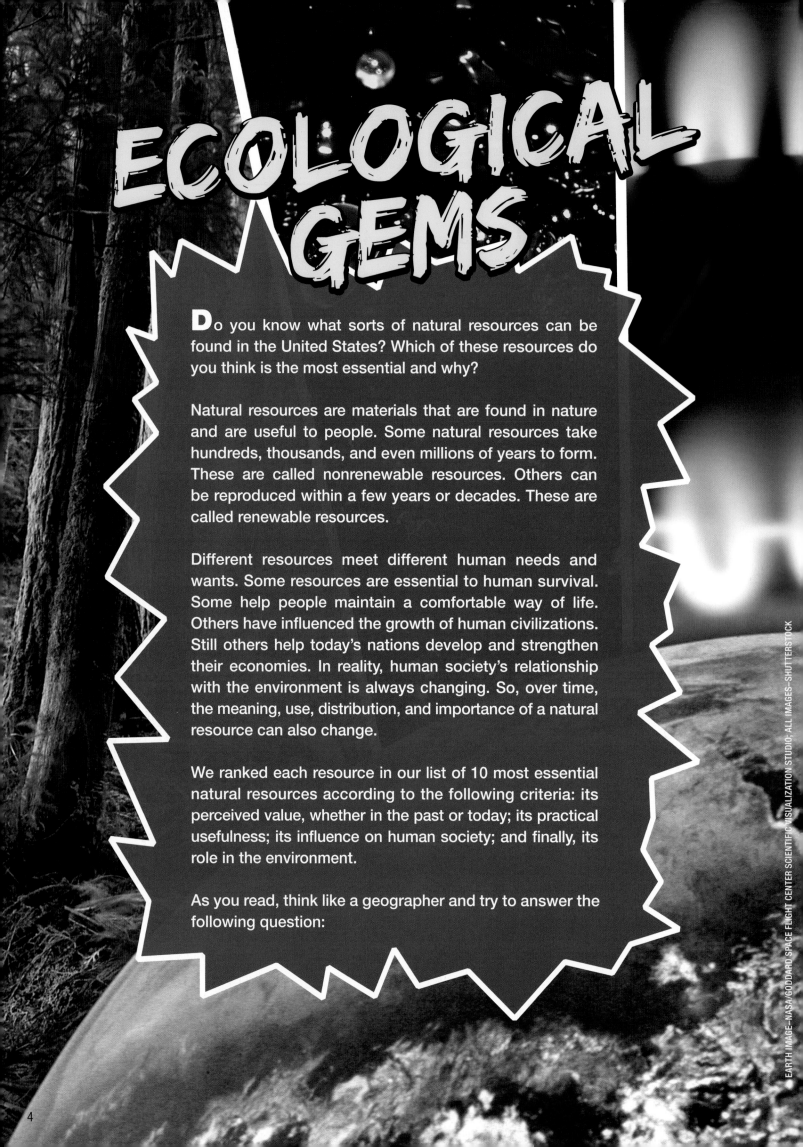

ECOLOGICAL GEMS

Do you know what sorts of natural resources can be found in the United States? Which of these resources do you think is the most essential and why?

Natural resources are materials that are found in nature and are useful to people. Some natural resources take hundreds, thousands, and even millions of years to form. These are called nonrenewable resources. Others can be reproduced within a few years or decades. These are called renewable resources.

Different resources meet different human needs and wants. Some resources are essential to human survival. Some help people maintain a comfortable way of life. Others have influenced the growth of human civilizations. Still others help today's nations develop and strengthen their economies. In reality, human society's relationship with the environment is always changing. So, over time, the meaning, use, distribution, and importance of a natural resource can also change.

We ranked each resource in our list of 10 most essential natural resources according to the following criteria: its perceived value, whether in the past or today; its practical usefulness; its influence on human society; and finally, its role in the environment.

As you read, think like a geographer and try to answer the following question:

EARTH IMAGE–NASA/GODDARD SPACE FLIGHT CENTER SCIENTIFIC VISUALIZATION STUDIO; ALL IMAGES–SHUTTERSTOCK

FIND GOLD

WHICH NATURAL RESOURCE IS THE MOST ESSENTIAL OF ALL?

Gold is called a "precious metal" because it is rare and very valuable.

WHAT IT IS: A soft, yellow metal; a nonrenewable resource

NATURALLY FOUND: Fixed in solid rock within or near the surface of Earth's crust

USES: Gold is used to make jewelry, money, dental materials, and electronic products.

Back in ancient times, gold was one of the first metals that people used for ornaments. It wasn't long before gold became a symbol of beauty, wealth, and power. People all over the world began to travel across continents and oceans looking for gold. Entire countries even went to war over it.

But what exactly makes this rare metal so precious? Well, it has many distinctive qualities that make it attractive and valuable to humans. It never loses its color and shine. Nor does it corrode, rust, or tarnish. Not only is gold beautiful, but it is also very useful. It is soft yet dense and can be hammered into thin sheets or drawn into fine wires. In addition, gold conducts, or carries, heat and electricity better than most other metals.

More gold is being mined right now than at any other time in history. It continues to have an impact on society, the economy, and the environment.

corrode: *dissolve or wear away*
dense: *heavy in relation to its size*

GOLD

A miner sifting for gold

WHERE ON EARTH?

The two main types of gold deposits are lode and placer (plass-ur). With lode deposits, the gold is found in cracks inside ore. Miners drill and blast the ore out of the ground and treat it with chemicals to remove the gold. With placer deposits, the gold has already been loosened from the rock by years of erosion. Bits of gold are often found mixed in sand, gravel, or rock. Miners simply sift or wash placer deposits with water to separate the gold.

IRREPLACEABLE

Since ancient times, people have been using gold to make ornaments and jewelry. Later, many nations began using gold as a form of money. Today, there is a growing demand for gold in electronics, manufacturing, and dentistry.

ore: *rock from which a valuable substance can be extracted*

? Compare the different uses of gold. Which do you think has the most impact on its price and why?

Quick Fact

With hard-rock mining, about nine tons of ore must be dug up and treated to produce about one ounce of gold.

CHANGE THE WORLD

The search for gold has had an effect on where humans move and settle. In the 1500s, Spanish conquistadors seeking gold overthrew the Aztec and Inca empires that used to rule what is now Central and South America. In the 1800s, gold rushes led people to Canada, the United States, Australia, New Zealand, and South Africa. New towns, cities, and mining industries emerged as a result of these rushes.

Today, gold mining is an industrial, large-scale operation. Although it still influences settlement patterns, it is having even more of an effect on the environment. Hard-rock mining can damage landscapes, and chemical treatment of ore can pollute land and water.

conquistadors: *leaders in the Spanish conquest of America and especially of Mexico and Peru in the 16th century*

? Should changes be made to how gold is mined? Consider the issue from the points of view of mining companies, mining workers, environmentalists, and the members of a community where a mine is located.

The Expert Says...

" Fascination, obsession, and aggression provoked by this strange and unique metal have shaped the destiny of humanity through the ages. "

— Peter L. Bernstein, author of *The Power of Gold: The History of an Obsession*

provoked: *stirred up*

Pure gold is too soft for practical use. So, it is often melted and mixed with another metal to make it harder.

10   9   8   7   6

KLONDIKE GOLD RUSH

Thousands of gold seekers flocked north to the Yukon and Alaska between 1897 and 1898. They were looking for gold near the Klondike River. Only a few of them found riches, but many stayed to start a new life in the north. By the time the gold rush came to an end in the 1900s, it had turned Dawson City, Yukon, and Skagway, Alaska, into boomtowns. Check out these two newspaper clippings from the days of the famous Klondike Gold Rush …

New York Gets It
Post–Intelligencer, July 19, 1897

NEW YORK — This city has been touched with the Alaskan gold fever. The past 24 hours has seen come to the front at least 2,000 [people] who will be on the way to the Klondike region just as soon as arrangements can be made for transportation. …

Quick Fact

Gold rushes often create boomtowns — towns that see a sudden growth in business and population. These boomtowns can grow into cities and centers of shipping, commerce, and manufacturing.

Died for a Nugget: An Eastern Klondiker Loses His Life in a Mining Shaft
Seattle Times, October 6, 1897

The fact that mining on the Klondike is dangerous at certain stages of the work and at certain times of the year, and that it has even resulted in [death], seems to have been overlooked in the lust for gold. In several instances, men have perished in their eagerness. …

perished: *died*

Skagway, Alaska

Take Note

Gold secures the #10 spot on our list. It is rare and has many useful qualities, making it a highly sought-after precious metal. The early hunt for gold had an impact on migratory and settlement patterns. But gold is only valued by humans and isn't essential to other animal or plant life.
- Some experts say that if there were more gold available in nature, it would be considered less precious. What do you think? Explain.

2   1

(9) DIAMONDS

The ancient Romans believed diamonds were pieces of fallen stars.

WHAT IT IS: An extremely hard crystal; a nonrenewable resource

NATURALLY FOUND: Fixed in rock within or near the surface of Earth's crust

USES: Diamonds are used in jewelry and in many industrial tools.

Once upon a time, diamonds were not nearly as valuable as they are today. In fact, in medieval times, most people actually preferred other gems to diamonds!

Diamonds were first found in ancient India. They were rare and exceptionally tough, and they often had a pleasing, delicate color. But besides polishing and shaping them with simple cuts, nobody really knew what else could be done with the gems. Then, in the 17th century, a gem expert from Italy discovered the "brilliant cut." It was a special way to cut a diamond that revealed its glitter and natural beauty. This discovery convinced the world that diamonds had major value.

Today, people all over the world pay large sums of money to buy diamond engagement rings or diamond-encrusted pieces of jewelry. And then there are those who are willing to pay the ultimate price — in some parts of the world, wars are being fought over this resource.

DIAMONDS

WHERE ON EARTH?

Diamonds are formed below Earth's crust. They are brought to the surface with magma during volcanic eruptions. Miners dig at the soil that forms after the magma has hardened and broken down. Many tons of solid rock, sand, and gravel must be mined and crushed to extract one small diamond. Erosion of volcanic soils over time leads to loose deposits in streambeds. These are called alluvial (uh-loo-vee-ul) diamonds.

Quick Fact

The world's first synthetic, or human-made, diamond was created in 1954. Synthetic diamonds are created in the lab. These are much cheaper than natural diamonds and are mostly used for industrial purposes.

IRREPLACEABLE

For many centuries, diamonds were used in their natural state as decorative gemstones. Today, the best diamonds are cut and crafted to make brilliant, glimmering jewels. The rest are used for industrial purposes. From mining to manufacturing, many industries rely on tools made with diamond to cut, drill, grind, or polish other hard materials.

magma: *molten rock*

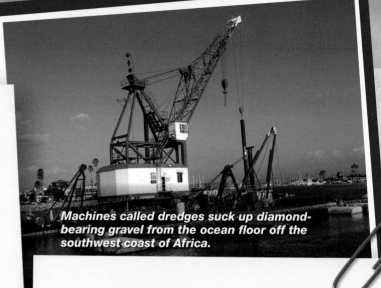

Machines called dredges suck up diamond-bearing gravel from the ocean floor off the southwest coast of Africa.

CHANGE THE WORLD

In the late 1860s, the discovery of the famous Kimberley fields in South Africa led to a major diamond rush. Within years, the diamond industry was fueling development throughout the area. In the late 1990s, armed conflicts broke out over the control of diamond mines in Angola, Sierra Leone, Liberia, and the Democratic Republic of Congo.

Diamond mining can result in land degradation, deforestation, and pollution. After an area is mined, the site is often left exposed, unsuitable for farming or any other activity.

development: *process of reaching higher levels of industrialization and standard of living*
degradation: *process of being worn down by erosion*

Why do you think people prefer natural diamonds over synthetic ones for jewelry?

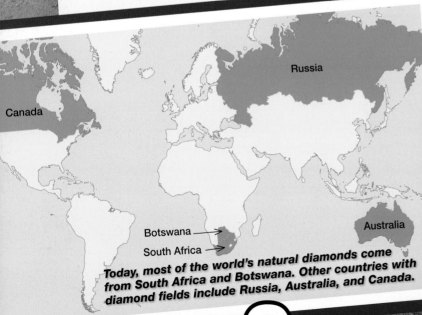

Canada

Russia

Botswana

South Africa

Australia

Today, most of the world's natural diamonds come from South Africa and Botswana. Other countries with diamond fields include Russia, Australia, and Canada.

The Expert Says...

Even if gems [or diamonds] are not linked to the initiation of conflict, there is good evidence that they tend to lengthen preexisting conflicts.

— Michael Ross, Department of Political Science, University of California

initiation: *start; introduction*

DIAMOND MINERS CRUELLY EXPLOITED

A newspaper article from the *Toronto Star*
By Michelle Glavic, February 14, 2007

Diamonds used to be a girl's best friend. Today they're everybody's best friend. ... Their beauty, elegance, and charm have captivated the world; diamonds make a statement. But there's a dark side to diamonds.

A few years ago very few people knew about blood diamonds, but now they're being publicized around the world in movies, songs, and newspapers. ...

[Diamond miners], who are only men, work in polluted water, receive very little pay and barely a cup of rice to eat each day. A miner suspected of stealing a diamond is executed immediately. If they find a rough diamond, they get paid a miniscule fraction of what it's really worth. One worker sold a diamond for $2.00, even though it was worth around $500.00. ...

In Sierra Leone, the workers were controlled by merciless rebels, the Revolutionary United Front or the RUF. ... All of the profits from the diamonds were used to buy weaponry, hence the name "conflict diamonds."

Diamond mining in Moa River, Sierra Leone

Today, many organizations and charities are reducing the number of blood diamonds being exported to Western countries. ... We still have a lot of work to do to totally exterminate blood diamonds from our market, but we've come a long way. ...

Michelle Glavic is an eighth-grade student in Niagara Falls, Ontario.

captivated: *enchanted; fascinated*
blood diamonds: *diamonds illegally traded to fund conflict in war-torn areas, and often linked to human rights abuses*
miniscule: *very small*
merciless: *cruel*

? Today, the diamond industry says it makes sure diamonds aren't from conflict areas. But critics say this promise means nothing if there is no independent party to monitor the industry. What more should be done about this issue?

Take Note

Diamonds take the #9 spot. As with gold, the rarity and beauty of diamonds make them highly sought-after for decorative purposes. Diamonds also have many industrial uses. Diamonds of high quality are sold for such great amounts of money that people are willing to fight, kill, and even die for them.
• Both gold and diamonds have been the cause of major conflicts around the world. How should we rethink the way we acquire, manage, and use these two natural resources? Explain.

5   3   2   1

8 NATURAL GAS

*Natural gas is an important fuel —
it supplies nearly 25 percent of the
energy used in the United States.*

WHAT IT IS: A flammable gas that is a mix of mostly methane and other gases; a nonrenewable resource

NATURALLY FOUND: Deep within Earth's crust

USES: Natural gas is used mainly as a fuel and as a raw material.

Geologists say that natural gas has been forming deep within the planet for hundreds of millions of years. It started with plant and animal remains that became buried in layers of rocks. Over time, intense heat and pressure, as well as chemical reactions, changed these trapped remains. They eventually became natural gas and crude oil — two forms of petroleum, which is the most important fossil fuel in the world.

Today, the countries producing the most natural gas include the United States and Canada. In the United States, production comes from the Gulf of Mexico and Louisiana, New Mexico, Oklahoma, Texas, and Wyoming. In Canada, production comes from Alberta, British Columbia, and offshore from Nova Scotia.

The world depends on natural gas to help meet its energy needs. As human populations continue to grow, natural gas will become even more valuable.

geologists: *scientists who study the origin, history, and structure of the earth*
producing: *extracting and processing in order to sell*

NATURAL GAS

Natural gas can be produced on every continent except Antarctica.

WHERE ON EARTH?

Natural gas can be extracted from Earth's crust through natural openings or drilled wells. Prospectors first study the geology of an area to find reserves of natural gas. Drilling crews then construct an exploratory well for geologists to test and evaluate a deposit. If the deposit contains a significant amount of natural gas, drillers complete the well and extract the gas. Today, natural gas is also drawn from coal mines and minor sources such as swamps, landfills, and waste processing plants.

IRREPLACEABLE

Natural gas is an important, efficient, and relatively clean source of energy. We burn natural gas to generate heat and electricity. Many industries also use the chemicals in natural gas to make detergents, drugs, plastics, and other products.

geology: *physical characteristics of an area, including its rocks, soils, and other features*
complete: *finish work on a well to prepare it for production*

CHANGE THE WORLD

Over the last century, hundreds of natural gas wells and more than a million miles of pipeline have been built in North America. Today, extensive pipelines are being built in Asia to meet growing energy demands. The international pipelines run east and south from Russia and Kazakhstan, north from Australia and Indonesia, and west from Alaska.

The burning of natural gas produces harmful gases, such as carbon dioxide. But natural gas is relatively cleaner than other fossil fuels. Because of this, the demand for natural gas continues to grow.

? Find out more about other forms of nonrenewable energy and how they compare to natural gas. Which would you recommend for use and why?

The Expert Says...

" Only decades ago, the fuel was viewed as nothing more than a pesky by-product of petroleum, a nuisance that made it more difficult to extract the 'black gold' underneath. Now natural gas itself has become a kind of gold. "

— Sam Williams, journalist

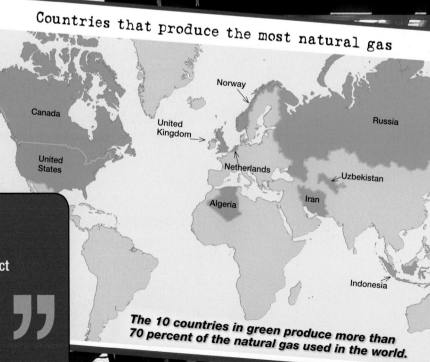

Countries that produce the most natural gas

Norway
Canada
United Kingdom
Russia
United States
Netherlands
Uzbekistan
Algeria
Iran
Indonesia

The 10 countries in green produce more than 70 percent of the natural gas used in the world.

10   9   **8**   7   6

Gas Up!

From beneath the ground to the storage tank, the journey of natural gas goes through four main stages. Check out this flowchart for more information.

1) Exploring

Prospectors work with geology experts to study an area to see whether there is gas. The only sure way to find out whether gas is present is to drill an exploratory well.

Drilling into seabeds is called offshore drilling.

2) Producing

Gas is produced by drilling wells either on land or into seabeds. The natural pressure of the deposit will force the gas up out of the ground and into the well.

3) Transmitting and Distributing

Before it is distributed, raw natural gas must be cleaned and treated. Processed natural gas is then fed into pipelines and carried to various communities along their routes. Pipelines are usually buried to minimize the risk of vandalism or accidental damage.

4) Storing

Neither individual consumers nor manufacturing industries use natural gas at a constant rate. So, gas is stored and later redistributed to meet changing demands.

? Do some research to find out more about each of these stages. Which do you think is the most expensive and why?

Take Note

Natural gas seeps into the #8 spot on our list. This fossil fuel is one of the world's most important sources of energy. It is relatively clean and can be used for a variety of purposes. The gas industry is building more pipelines and digging more wells around the world to meet the increasing demand for this valuable resource.
• Why is the expert knowledge of scientists so essential to prospectors?

Quick Fact

Pure natural gas is odorless. Before distributing the gas, utility companies add chemicals to it to give it a strong smell. Gas leaks are then easier to detect, preventing serious accidents.

5   4   3   2   1

(7) COAL

At one point in time, coal was called "black diamond" because it was so valuable.

WHAT IT IS: A black, combustible rock; a nonrenewable resource

NATURALLY FOUND: Within Earth's crust

USES: Coal is widely used as a fuel.

There was a time in the history of the planet, about 250 million years ago, when an unusually large amount of coal began to form. Good thing, too, since humans have come to rely heavily on coal for power. In fact, the mining industry digs up about 3.5 billion tons of coal around the world every year!

Coal was formed from ancient bogs where plants grew densely. When these plants died, their remains built up in the waters of the bogs. These decaying plants gradually turned into something called peat. As layer after layer of plant remains formed, deposits of peat began to sink deeper into the bogs. Then, over time, many of these ancient bogs were covered by sand and mud. Buried well below the ground, the peat deposits were gradually transformed into coal by intense pressure and heat.

Coal might not be as outwardly impressive as shiny nuggets of gold or glimmering bits of diamond, but these combustible lumps of black rock are actually a lot more valuable to humankind. Read on to find out why coal is #7 on our list.

bogs: *areas of wet spongy ground, consisting mainly of decayed or decaying plant matter*
combustible: *capable of burning*

COAL

An old mining cart

WHERE ON EARTH?

Underground mines are dug to extract deposits deep within Earth's crust. If the coal is found close to the surface, a technique called strip mining is used. Strip mining removes the top layers of soil and rock to expose the coal. In many parts of the world, the best and most accessible coal has already been mined.

? If the best and most accessible coal has already been mined in many parts of the world, will the resource's value change? Why or why not?

IRREPLACEABLE

Coal is used as a fuel to provide heat and generate electricity. A by-product of coal, called coke, is used to melt iron ore to make steel. Chemicals that come from coal are used to make materials such as plastics, nylon, drugs, dyes, and fertilizers.

CHANGE THE WORLD

It was not until the late 1700s, with the start of the Industrial Revolution, that people began to rely on and value coal. Coal was needed to power the steam engines that were used in ships, locomotives, and factories. Historians say nations that lacked coal fell behind in economic and industrial development.

Coal mining can produce waste, scar the landscape, and contaminate the surrounding environment. The burning of coal pollutes the air.

Industrial Revolution: *period marked by important changes in society, when hand tools and home manufacturing were replaced by power-driven tools and large-scale factory production*

Quick Fact

There are three types of coal: low-quality coal is mainly burned at power plants for electricity; mid-quality coal is used in the steel and iron industry because it burns the hottest; and the highest quality coal is used in homes because it produces the least smoke and pollution.

Underground mines are dug to reach coal deposits that are deeper than 200 feet below Earth's surface.

The Expert Says...

" Energy-wise, the fundamental problem in the world today is that Earth's reserves of fossil fuels are finite, but our appetite is not. "

— Jeff Goodell, author of *Big Coal: The Dirty Secret Behind America's Energy Future*

finite: *limited*

BLACK LUNG

Black lung is a serious and often fatal disease. It is caused by years of breathing coal mine dust. Find out more by reading the list of facts and quotations below ...

● Black lung used to be called "miner's asthma." Today, it is known as coal workers' pneumoconiosis (noo-moe-coe-nee-o-sis). In 1969, studies found that 40 to 60 percent of miners had black lung. The numbers have dropped in recent years, but it is still a common condition in the industry.

● Symptoms of black lung include breathing problems, frequent coughing, and black spit. In serious cases, a patient's lungs can become scarred and blackened.

● There is no treatment for black lung — the damage cannot be undone. Prevention, by making sure miners are not inhaling the dust as they work, is the only way to combat this disease.

"The dust was so thick sometimes you couldn't see your hand in front of you, even with your light. You just spit it up. You just live in it."

— Connie Cline, former miner from West Virginia

"Unfortunately, black lung disease is not likely to disappear. ... [T]his will be the hidden disaster. These deaths won't hit the headlines and will take place quietly decades from now."

— Robert Cohen, director, black lung clinic, Chicago

Coal dust can spread throughout the lungs and show up as tiny spots on an X-ray.

Take Note

Coal takes the #7 spot. It played a huge role in powering the Industrial Revolution. Even today, it is still an important source of heat and energy. It is cheap, accessible, and relatively abundant. But as useful as it may be, the mining and burning of this "dirty" fossil fuel can damage the environment and harm our health.
• Do the benefits of coal outweigh the drawbacks? Should the mining and use of coal be banned? Why or why not?

? Various health and safety dangers still exist in the coal-mining industry. What can the industry do to better protect miners? Explain.

5   4   3   2   1

The world's oil supply will not last forever. A limited amount of oil exists beneath the ground.

WHAT IT IS: A thick, flammable, yellow-to-black liquid; a nonrenewable resource

NATURALLY FOUND: Deep within Earth's crust, or near the surface in oil sands

USES: Oil is used mainly as a fuel, but is also an important raw material for many industrial purposes.

Without oil, our modern way of life would be impossible. Most of the things that make our lives more comfortable and convenient either run on oil or are made from oil. This should be no surprise. Oil has many more uses than any other substance in the world.

It was not always like this. In the early 1800s, people digging wells for water often struck oil. But instead of thinking that they had struck it rich, they were disappointed and even disgusted. They usually abandoned their wells because at the time there was no demand for this sticky, smelly substance they called "rock oil."

Then, in the mid-1800s, a chemist's findings changed everything. Benjamin Silliman reported that oil was not as worthless as everyone thought it was. In fact, it could be used to make many products, including lamp oils, lubricating oils, and wax. Historians call Silliman's report a milestone in the history of oil. It convinced people that profitable businesses could be developed with this natural resource.

OIL

Oil can be extracted from underground reservoirs by using a pump jack, such as the one seen here.

WHERE ON EARTH?

Most petroleum lies in underground formations called traps. In a trap, oil collects in the spaces within or between solid rock. Crews drill or dig a hole in the ground so that the oil can either flow out on its own or be pumped out. Oil can also be extracted from oil sands by surface mining. Oil sands are a mixture of sand, water, and heavy oil. Oil sands can be so soaked with oil that workers get their hands oily just by handling them.

IRREPLACEABLE

People have used oil to make adhesives, lubricants, ointments, construction materials, and fuel for lamps. Today, oil is the source of nearly all fuels used for transportation, such as gasoline, diesel fuel, and jet fuel. Other oil-based fuels generate heat and electric power. Oil is also an important raw material. It is the main ingredient in plastics. It is also used in a variety of products such as cosmetics, cleaners, fertilizers, and greases.

> **?** Many products today are made of plastic, instead of wood or metal. What are the benefits and drawbacks of this? Explain your answer.

CHANGE THE WORLD

Oil has powered nearly every industry in modern history. Control of oil supplies even influenced the course of World Wars I and II. The unequal distribution of the world's oil resources has long been and will continue to be the source of international conflicts.

Besides causing political and social instability, drilling for oil disturbs land and ocean habitats. Producing and moving oil often leads to leaks and spills that pollute rivers and oceans. Refining and burning oil pollutes the air.

refining: *making pure; removing unwanted matter from*

The Expert Says...

" Petroleum has had a critical role in helping to develop today's technological and industrial capacity … . The almost total reliance on oil and natural gas for key aspects of modern life was a necessary stage of human development. "

— Bilaal Abdullah, author of *Peak Oil Paradigm Shift: The Urgent Need for a Sustainable Energy Model*

> **?** Do you agree with what the expert says about the role of petroleum in modern society? Give examples to support your answer.

Quick Fact

During World War I, oil became a key military asset due to the adoption of oil-powered ships, airplanes, and vehicles such as trucks and tanks. During World War II, nations fought battles for the control of petroleum-producing regions.

From the EXPERTS

Check out these quotations to hear what three experts on the oil industry have to say about the importance of oil.

"Black gold" has turned many rags to riches, for individuals and for nations. It has spawned jealousies and arrogance, and has been a key factor in several wars ... .

— C. J. Campbell, author of *Oil Crisis*

In the fast-moving world of oil politics, oil is not simply a source of world power, but a medium for that power as well, a substance whose huge importance enmeshes companies, communities, and entire nations in a taut global web ... .

— Paul Roberts, author of *The End of Oil: On the Edge of a Perilous New World*

medium: *means by which something is expressed or achieved*
taut: *tightly drawn; tense*

? What do you think will begin to happen to this "taut global web" as oil resources become depleted? Explain your answer.

The use of oil has changed world economies, social and political structures, and lifestyles beyond the effect of any other substance in such a short time.

— Walter Youngquist, author of *GeoDestinies: The inevitable control of Earth resources over nations and individuals*

Quick Fact
About 65 percent of the world's known oil reserves are located in the Middle East. The export of oil is the most important way of generating revenue for countries in this region.

Take Note
Oil slides into the #6 spot on our list. Hands down, it is one of modern society's most important natural resources. It is an essential source of fuel and power. Its widespread use and dwindling supply combine to make oil one of the most sought-after resources today.
• How can individuals, businesses, and nations prepare for the day when oil supplies run out?

5   **4**   **3**   **2**   **1**

5 IRON

Iron is a metal that can be used to make durable and precise tools, weapons, and other items.

IRON ORE–© JAMES L. AMOS/CORBIS

WHAT IT IS: A hard, silvery-white metal; a nonrenewable resource

NATURALLY FOUND: Within Earth's crust

USES: Iron is used to make steel, which is essential to many major industries, including manufacturing, mining, construction, transportation, and agriculture.

Over the course of time, iron has come to be associated with everything that is firm, strong, and healthy. Think about it. We admire the unrelenting determination of people who have a "will of iron" or "iron resolve." We describe leaders who hold tightly to their position of power as having an "iron grip." We applaud the great endurance of athletes who compete in "ironman competitions."

So how, or when, did iron achieve such a powerful image? This plain-looking metal does not seem nearly as precious as gold or silver, but iron has had greater influence on human history than any other metal on the planet. People have been using iron to make tools and weapons since prehistoric times. Learning how to melt and hammer iron to create better tools has allowed human civilizations to develop and reshape the world.

unrelenting: *firm; not giving up*

IRON

An open-pit mine

WHERE ON EARTH?

Iron is one of the most widely distributed and abundant elements in Earth's crust. Iron ore near the surface is extracted by digging an open pit. To reach deep deposits, a shaft is sunk so that miners can dig tunnels to the ore.

IRREPLACEABLE

About 90 percent of the iron that is extracted in the world is used to make steel. Steel is used to make tools, utensils, and weapons, as well as automobiles, aircraft, heavy machinery, electronics, and satellites. Iron is also made directly into cast-iron products such as pipes and hydrants. Wrought-iron products include furniture and decorative ironwork.

> **?** The Industrial Revolution changed the Western world from a rural, agricultural society to an urban, industrial society. What have been some of the benefits and problems of industrialization?

Hot steel

CHANGE THE WORLD

When people in different parts of the world learned to use iron to make tools, the Iron Age began. Tools made with iron were stronger, sharper, and more durable than tools made with stone or bronze. This dramatically improved farming, woodworking, transportation, and other areas of life. With the Industrial Revolution, iron became an important raw material for tools and equipment used in growing industries. More recently, steel has been the foundation of the modern automobile, building construction, and various consumer-goods industries.

Mining iron ore has many negative impacts on the environment. At mine sites, vegetation is destroyed and the natural landscape is changed completely. The extraction and processing of iron ore produce large amounts of waste material. Smelting and refining can result in air pollution.

smelting: *melting ore to separate the metal*

> **?** An element of nature, such as iron, is only a "resource" if it is of use to humans. Do you think iron will ever lose its value and status as a natural resource? Why or why not?

The Expert Says...

"Iron was the great equalizer: any people could now be self-sufficient. A nation no longer needed rare natural resources, hoarded capital, a developed trading apparatus, or even civilization to compete as a great power. The Iron Age saw new nations rise ... ."

— Geoffrey Bibby, The Prehistoric Museum, Denmark

apparatus: *means by which a function or task is performed*

10   **9**   **8**   **7**   **6**

The Iron Age

The Iron Age was the period in history when communities around the world began to use tools and weapons made of iron. This timeline tracks the development of this important age:

3500 – 3000 B.C.
People in the ancient Middle East and Egypt begin to smelt iron ore and use iron to make simple tools.

1900 – 1600 B.C.
People in Asia Minor, a peninsula between the Black and Mediterranean seas, begin to smelt iron ore. They refine the iron to create alloys and useful objects.

1000 B.C.
Iron objects and the art of iron forging gradually spreads throughout the Middle East, the Mediterranean region, and the rest of Europe.

600 B.C.
The Iron Age begins in China. Early iron objects include swords and other weapons. Iron is also used to make axes, hoes, and other equipment, revolutionizing agriculture in China.

500 B.C.
Forging iron tools and jewelry becomes widespread in Europe. Techniques developed at this time remain virtually unchanged until the Middle Ages.

400 B.C.
Large-scale iron production begins in parts of Africa. Ironworking spreads to the rest of the continent within 100 years.

Quick Fact
Iron ore can be found all over the world. Areas with more than one billion tons of reserves include Australia, Brazil, Canada, China, India, South Africa, Sweden, and the United States.

Take Note
Iron takes the #5 spot on our list. It has been an essential natural resource for thousands of years. With iron, humankind has been able to forge tools and weapons. Then, with steel, humankind began to build different structures and forms of transportation. Useful, reliable, and long-lasting — iron is an essential resource, no doubt about it.
- The Iron Age is the third of three ages (Stone, Bronze, and Iron) into which the early history of humankind is typically divided. What age are we in now? Which natural resource is at the center of human development today? Explain.

ALL IMAGES–SHUTTERSTOCK AND ISTOCKPHOTO.

5   4   3   2   1

4 SALT

Salt companies produce more than 300 types of salts for different uses.

WHAT IT IS: A clear, brittle mineral; a nonrenewable resource

NATURALLY FOUND: In the ground, or dissolved in the oceans, seas, and saltwater lakes

USES: Salt is used to flavor and preserve food; it is also an important raw material for the chemical industry.

Most people know that you cannot survive for more than a few days without food and water. But did you know that you also cannot survive without salt? Humans need some salt for their bodies to function properly. Without salt, the body can become dangerously dehydrated — salt actually helps the body retain water.

Its importance to human health isn't the only reason why salt is considered an extremely valuable natural resource. Salt is an essential ingredient in everything from French fries to fabric dyes, water softeners to window cleaners. No wonder more and more salt is being collected from nature every year!

SALT

Rock salt

WHERE ON EARTH?

The original source of salt is brine, or salty water, from ancient seas and salt lakes. When these seas dried up millions of years ago, large deposits of salt were left behind. These deposits are called salt beds or rock salt. They are found all over the world, buried beneath layers of rocks. Salt miners dig into the ground to reach a deposit and then use explosives to blast the salt loose. Salt is also obtained by evaporating salt water from seas and lakes.

Quick Fact

Salt was so important in the Middle Ages that the salt trade was often in the control of rulers or leaders. In many countries, no one was allowed to mine or sell salt without permission from the government.

IRREPLACEABLE

In ancient times, salt was used as medicine and a form of money. For thousands of years, it has been widely used in seasoning and preserving food. Today, the biggest users of salt are chemical companies. When broken down, the mineral is a key component of different products, including paper, plastic, glass, fabric dyes, cleaners, pesticides, water softeners, deicers, and antifreeze.

CHANGE THE WORLD

Being able to preserve food meant that people could travel long distances, and away from farmlands, without fear of starving. Many of the world's first roads, trade routes, and canals were used for transporting salt. Many great cities, from Venice to Genoa, Liverpool to Timbuktu, began as centers of the salt trade. Once people learned to boil brine to obtain salt, many of them settled around brine springs — these settlements became early towns and cities.

Early methods and technology used in salt exploration and mining paved the way for other mining-based activities, including the search for petroleum.

brine springs: *small streams of salt water flowing naturally from the ground*

Salt makes up almost 80 percent of the dissolved solids in ocean water. Salt is in even higher concentration in inland seas and saltwater lakes.

The Expert Says...

Salt is such a common part of our everyday existence that we rarely think of it as a natural resource that must be discovered, mined, processed, and marketed. Yet salt is so vital to our lives that without it we could perish.

— Natural Resources Canada

Besides salt, what is another resource that most people take for granted because it is such a common part of everyday life?

Salt Revolution

How did salt help determine the fate of India in the mid-20th century? This account describes the country's fight for freedom from foreign rule ...

The leader of India's fight for independence from the British Empire was Mohandas Gandhi. He believed in nonviolent resistance. To protest unpopular and unfair British laws, he went on hunger strikes, pushed for boycotts, and organized massive marches. One of these marches — the Salt March — came to be seen as India's first step toward freedom.

In 1930, Gandhi led a march to the coast of Dandi, Gujarat, to illegally make salt from seawater. He wanted to openly defy British salt laws. At the time, even though India had large reserves of natural rock salt, British laws forced the Indian people to buy their salt from British-owned companies.

Mohandas Gandhi and thousands of supporters marched for almost a month to defy British salt laws.

On April 5, after walking more than 240 miles, Gandhi finally arrived at the seashore. Taking up a lump of salty mud, Gandhi declared, "With this, I am shaking the foundations of the British Empire."

Gandhi's act of defiance inspired millions of people across India to break the salt laws as well. Some made their own salt; others bought illegal salt. The Salt March and other actions shook up the entire country. Massive nonviolent protests continued. In 1947, India succeeded in gaining full independence from British rule.

Protesters broke salt laws by filling containers with seawater.

Take Note

Salt ranks #4 on our list. It is used for preserving and preparing food. The salt trade created wealth and played a role in the early development of major cities around the world. Today, salt is used in greater quantities and for more applications than any other mineral. It is also essential to human health.

• Salt is useful and valuable for many different reasons. Yet it costs very little to buy. Why do you think this is?

5   4   3   2   1

③ TREES

Most trees will grow to large sizes and live for many years.

TREES—SHUTTERSTOCK

34

WHAT IT IS: Tall woody plants that have a single main stem or trunk; a renewable resource

NATURALLY FOUND: Widely distributed over most of the world's land surfaces except the coldest and driest parts

USES: Trees are vital to the natural environment; they also provide people with food, shelter, clothing, and fuel.

We couldn't live without trees. Trees provide us with wood, which we use to make countless essential products. From the paper for this book to the wood in your pencil and the chair you might be sitting on, many everyday items came from trees. Trees also provide wildlife with food and shelter. And most importantly, trees play an essential role in helping sustain the natural environment. They filter the air and release oxygen; they hold soil in place; and they help maintain high-quality water supplies.

In many parts of the world, entire forests are being cut down without an adequate number of new trees being replanted. The consequences of deforestation can be devastating on a regional and global scale.

TREES

Trees can grow anywhere, as long as it is not too cold or too dry.

WHERE ON EARTH?

Thousands of different species of trees grow in nearly all parts of the world. In well-managed forests, a forester decides which trees loggers should cut within a forest. The decision to cut is determined by the species, age, and size of the trees. Today, trees are also grown as crops. Tree farms ensure that there will be an ample supply of trees available while preserving wildlife habitats and ensuring the conservation of natural forests.

IRREPLACEABLE

Trees provide foods, medicines, and wood. We use wood to make thousands of products, from timber that is used for construction, to pulp that is turned into paper, to firewood that is burned for fuel. Trees protect soils from erosion and are valuable wildlife habitats. They also help maintain the balance of gases in the air by absorbing carbon dioxide and releasing oxygen.

forester: *person who is trained to manage forests*

CHANGE THE WORLD

For thousands of years, trees have played a crucial role in human progress. Since prehistoric times, people have used trees to build homes and other structures, make tools and weapons, and create different forms of transportation. Logging was one of the first industries in the developing world. About 1.5 million years ago, humans began using wood as a fuel to make fire.

? What factors have led to the changing value and importance of trees over time?

Overharvesting of trees destroys wildlife habitats, which can drive some species to extinction.

The Expert Says...

" [C]onserving forests, growing forests, and replanting forests … will not only help with climate change, if well-planned they also can provide habitat for wildlife and help build conservation-based economies. "

— Stewart Elgie, associate director, Institute of the Environment, University of Ottawa

10   9   8   6

Resource Recovery

Read this report to find out how a practice called resource recovery can help conserve the world's natural supply of trees.

Although natural ecological cycles can replace renewable resources over time, we still have to use these resources in a sustainable way. When it comes to trees, we can try to plant more to replace the ones we have cut down. But overharvesting and overconsumption threaten to deplete the world's natural supply of trees.

Today, many people say we are not doing enough to conserve trees. A new practice called resource recovery should help. Australia and New Zealand are already trying it out. There, builders look for reusable materials from old wooden structures, such as old buildings, bridges, and wharves. They even salvage wood found on the bottom of lakes. Recovered wood can be used to make such things as furniture, floorboards, and ceiling beams.

When a company uses recovered wood, it saves materials that would otherwise be wasted. It also helps to conserve energy and avoid creating the pollution that would have resulted from the harvesting and processing of living trees.

---

sustainable: *capable of being continued with minimal long-term effect on the environment*
deplete: *use up*

Quick Fact

Forests that have never been logged are called old-growth forests. It takes many generations for an old-growth forest to mature, and so, old-growth trees are actually considered a nonrenewable resource.

Take Note

Trees come in at #3. They are essential to humans because they provide such a wide variety of useful products. Wildlife also relies on trees to survive. Even the environment would be very different without trees — they are vital to keeping air, water, and soil clean and healthy.
• How can we make better use of this natural resource? Create a flowchart to show how many different uses you can get out of a single tree.

5   4   **3**   2   1

Many forms of human activity — including urban development, agriculture, mining, and waste disposal — can harm the quality of soil.

WHAT IT IS: A loose mixture of minerals, plant and animal matter, and air and water; a nonrenewable resource

NATURALLY FOUND: On Earth's surface

USES: Soils are used for crop production, road and building construction, and even waste disposal; many living organisms find shelter in soil.

How essential is soil? Well, plainly and simply: There would be no life on land without soil.

Soil covers much of Earth's surface. But even if it seems plentiful, fertile soil is actually a very fragile and limited resource. It takes many years to develop but can be quickly and easily destroyed by human activity. Soil is constantly lost as humans expand towns and cities. Houses, factories, and roads are often built over fertile land.

What's more, soil hardly needs to be bulldozed or paved over to lose its ability to support life. Even if it is simply mismanaged, it will lose many of the properties that make it essential. Careless management allows soil to be blown away by wind or washed away by rain, leaving us with less and less fertile land on which to grow crops. Turn the page to find out just how devastating the consequences can be when we misuse this natural resource.

fertile: *capable of supporting plant life, especially crops*

SOIL

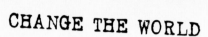

WHERE ON EARTH?

Soil is found in layers, called horizons, on Earth's surface. The bottom layer consists of parent material, or the loose organic and mineral matter that is broken down to form soil. Above this is subsoil, which is low in organic matter. The next is topsoil, which is rich in the nutrients that plants need to grow. At the very top are dead leaves, twigs, and other organic materials that are just beginning to decay.

IRREPLACEABLE

Most life on land relies on soil as a direct or indirect source of food. Plants obtain nutrients from the soil in which they grow. In turn, humans and other animals get nutrients from these plants. Many creatures live in soil, and humans have also used soil as a material for building foundations and dams.

organic: *relating to living organisms*

CHANGE THE WORLD

The discovery that land could be used to produce food changed human society forever. Before, humans moved from place to place to hunt animals. Once people began farming and producing stable and large quantities of food, settlements grew in number and in size. These farming settlements became towns, which grew into cities over time. Even as the world keeps industrializing, the search continues for fertile land.

Soil can erode as a result of poor agricultural practices, clearing of forests, mining, industrial waste dumping, and improper disposal of urban wastes. If land is left bare, wind and rain may carry away topsoil — after that, it is gone forever.

Quick Fact

Experts estimate that only 12 percent of Earth's land can produce crops. The rest is too hot, too cold, too steep, too shallow, too wet, too dry, or too toxic.

The erosion of fertile land can be prevented. For instance, following the curve of the land when plowing slows down the flow of water and soil. Rotating crops every now and then prevents minerals in the soil from being exhausted.

The Expert Says...

"The thin layer of soil covering the Earth's surface represents the difference between survival and extinction for most terrestrial life."

— John W. Doran and Timothy B. Parkin, authors of *Defining and Assessing Soil Quality*

terrestrial: *living or growing on land*

? Today, construction sites are one of the biggest sources of soil erosion. If you were hired to monitor the industry, what methods would you recommend to reduce the amount of soil that washes and blows away?

THE DUST BOWL

DURING THE 1930s, A PART OF THE UNITED STATES TURNED INTO A GIANT DUST BOWL. FIND OUT EXACTLY WHAT HAPPENED IN THIS REPORT FROM THE LIBRARY OF CONGRESS.

Between 1930 and 1940, the south-western Great Plains region of the United States suffered a severe drought. Once a semi-arid grassland, the treeless plains became home to thousands of settlers. ... Most of the settlers farmed their land or grazed cattle. The farmers plowed the prairie grasses and planted wheat. As the demand for wheat products grew, cattle grazing was reduced, and millions more acres were plowed and planted.

Dryland farming on the Great Plains led to the systematic destruction of the prairie grasses. In the ranching regions, overgrazing also destroyed large areas of grassland. Gradually, the land was laid bare, and significant environmental damage began to occur. Among the natural elements, the strong winds of the region were particularly devastating.

With the onset of drought in 1930, the over-farmed and overgrazed land began to blow away. Winds whipped across the plains, raising billowing clouds of dust. The sky could darken for days, and even well-sealed homes could have a thick layer of dust on the furniture. In some places, the dust drifted like snow, covering farm buildings and houses. Nineteen states in the heartland of the United States became a vast dust bowl. With no chance of making a living, farm families abandoned their homes and land, fleeing westward to become migrant laborers.

Great Plains: *vast prairie region in the central United States*
semi-arid: *moderately dry climate, with slight amounts of rainfall*
dryland farming: *production of crops without irrigation*

The dust storms and sandstorms were so severe that entire roads and houses were buried. Clouds from these storms could be seen hundreds of miles away.

Take Note

Soil takes the #2 spot! Life on land depends on the existence of soil. It might seem as if there is soil everywhere, but fertile soil is actually a limited and fragile resource. This makes it very valuable and requires us to use it very wisely.

• Experts believe that soil will become even more valuable and important in the world as time goes by. Why do you think they would say this?

5   4   3   **2**   1

41 DUST STORM–NOAA GEORGE E. MARSH ALBUM, DUST COVERED TRACTOR–NATIONAL OCEANIC AND ATMOSPHERIC ADMINISTRATION/DEPARTMENT OF COMMERCE ALL IMAGES–SHUTTERSTOCK AND ISTOCK

1 FRESHWAT

Freshwater descends from the clouds as rain and forms lakes and streams.

ANGEL FALLS—GETTY IMAGES/MARK COSSLETT/NGS46_0433

ER

WHAT IT IS: A clear, colorless, odorless, and tasteless liquid; a renewable resource

NATURALLY FOUND: On Earth's surface, below the ground, and in the air

USES: Freshwater is essential for all terrestrial life.

Water permits life. Water sustains life. Water is life. It is by far the most essential natural resource on the planet. Nothing can take its place.

Throughout human history, access to freshwater has been a determining factor between life and death. Societies rise where supplies of freshwater are plentiful. They fall when these supplies dry up.

Water also changes the face of Earth. It wears down mountains, carves valleys, and cuts deep canyons. It also helps to control Earth's climate.

The challenge that faces humankind today is how to use freshwater in a sustainable way. As the world's population increases, more water will be needed than ever before. Unfortunately, pollution, mismanagement of supplies, and a changing climate are threatening to create serious global freshwater shortages. Are we ready to become better guardians of this essential resource?

FRESHWATER

WHERE ON EARTH?

Most of Earth's supply of water is in the oceans. However, ocean water is too salty for drinking, agriculture, and even industrial uses. Instead, humans require freshwater, which makes up about three percent of Earth's water. Two main sources of freshwater are surface water and groundwater. Rivers, lakes, and reservoirs are sources of surface water. Groundwater comes from aquifers (ah-qwuh-furs), which are tapped by digging or drilling wells.

IRREPLACEABLE

All terrestrial life needs freshwater to survive. We use huge amounts of freshwater to grow crops and raise livestock. People also use water for cleaning, cooking, and outdoor recreation. Water in sewers carries away wastes. Industries use water as a raw material and as a cleaning or cooling substance. Some power stations use water to produce electricity.

reservoirs: *human-made lakes*
aquifers: *underground layers of rock, sand, or gravel that contain trapped water*

Bottled water has become very popular. Find out more about its benefits and drawbacks. Is this a good or bad way of managing and using this resource?

Most of Earth's freshwater is locked in ice caps and glaciers.

CHANGE THE WORLD

The first human civilizations were all located near the world's greatest freshwater rivers. Numerous early civilizations formed in the region of Mesopotamia close to the Tigris and Euphrates rivers. Ancient Egypt flourished next to the Nile, and the ancient Chinese settled around the Yellow River. Throughout history, access to freshwater has determined whether humans can sustain their lifestyle and survive.

Today, freshwater supplies are in danger of being contaminated by pollutants such as human and other animal wastes, toxic chemicals, metals, and oils. Governments and industries are spending billions of dollars to reduce pollution and construct water treatment plants. A warming global climate is also threatening supplies — rivers, lakes, and aquifers are drying up. Water conservation is especially important for preventing serious shortages in freshwater supplies in the world.

Quick Fact

In 2003, the United Nations released a report warning of a worldwide water crisis. It said that by 2050, more than half of the world's population will be living with severe water shortages.

The Expert Says...

"The most valuable commodity in the world today, and likely to remain so for much of this century, is not oil, not natural gas, not even some type of renewable energy. It's water — clean, safe, freshwater."

— Larry West, environmental journalist

The Water Cycle

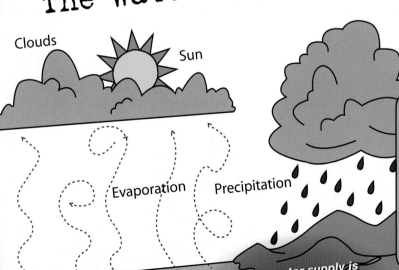

Clouds

Sun

Evaporation   Precipitation

Ocean

Earth's water supply is recycled and renewed by the water cycle.

Water Conservation:
Do Your Part!

Are you doing your part to help conserve Earth's supply of freshwater? Check out this fact chart to see how you can improve your water conservation habits.

Activity	Normal Use	Conservation Use
Washing Hands or Face	Water running: **2 gallons**	Plug and fill sink: **1 gallon**
Showering	Water running: **25 gallons**	Wet down; soap down; rinse: **4 gallons**
Bathing	Tub full: **40 gallons**	Minimal water level: **10 – 12 gallons**
Brushing Teeth	Tap running: **5 gallons**	Wet brush; turn water off; rinse: **½ gallon**

Activity	Normal Use	Conservation Use
Drinking	Run water to cool: **1 gallon**	Keep water in refrigerator: **8 ounces**
Dishwasher	Full cycle: **16 gallons**	Short cycle: **7 gallons**
Dishes by Hand	Tap running: **30 gallons**	Wash and rinse in sink: **5 gallons**
Washing Clothes	Full cycle, top water level: **60 gallons**	Short cycle, minimal water level: **27 gallons**

Adapted from the U.S. Dept of Agriculture, Natural Resources Conservation Service

In what other ways could freshwater be better used or conserved?

Take Note

Freshwater is the #1 most essential natural resource on Earth. It is life itself — it is a basic requirement for all living things on land. The first human civilizations all began next to Earth's mightiest freshwater rivers. The struggle to maintain freshwater supplies is one of the most important challenges to humankind today.

- Find out what experts are saying about looming freshwater shortages. What do you think needs to be done to avoid a potential disaster?

5   4   3   2   1

We Thought ...

Here are the criteria we used in ranking the 10 most essential natural resources.

The resource:
- Is useful to humans
- Has market value
- Has seen increased use over time
- Is used as a raw material to make other products
- Played a role in developing ancient human civilizations
- Influenced modern-day migratory or settlement patterns
- Has continually influenced the course of world history
- Is vital to plant and animal survival

What Do You Think?

1. Do you agree with our ranking? If you don't, try ranking the natural resources yourself. Justify your ranking with data from your own research and reasoning. You may refer to our criteria, or you may want to draw up your own list of criteria.

2. Here are three other natural resources that we considered but in the end did not include in our top 10 list: uranium, copper, and bauxite.
   - Find out more about these resources. Do you think they should have made our list? Give reasons for your response.
   - Are there other resources that you think should have made our list? Explain your choices.

Index

A

Abdullah, Bilaal, 24
Africa, 12, 29
Alaska, 9, 16
Angola, 12
Animal, 9, 15, 39–40, 44, 46
Asia, 16, 29
Australia, 8, 12, 16, 29, 37

B

Bauxite, 47
Bibby, Geoffrey, 28
Bernstein, Peter L., 8
Botswana, 12
Brazil, 29

C

Canada, 8, 12, 15, 29
Central America, 8
China, 29, 44
Coal, 16, 18–21
Conflict, 12–13, 24
Conservation, 36–37, 44–45
Copper, 47
Crop, 36, 39–41, 44

D

Dawson City, 9
Democratic Republic of Congo, 12
Development, 4, 12, 20, 23–24, 27–29, 33, 36, 38–39, 46
Diamonds, 10–13, 18–19
Doran, John W., 40
Dust bowl, 41

E

Economy, 4, 7, 20, 25, 36
Egypt, 29
Elgie, Stewart, 36
Energy, 14–17, 20–21, 24, 37, 44
Europe, 29
Extinction, 36, 40

F

Food, 31–33, 35–36, 40
Fossil fuel, 15–17, 20–21
Freshwater, 42–45

G

Gandhi, Mohandas, 33
Geology, 16–17
Gold, 6–9, 13, 16, 19, 25, 27
Goodell, Jeff, 20

I

India, 11, 29, 33
Indonesia, 16
Industrial Revolution, 20–21, 28
Industry, 8, 11–13, 16–17, 19–21, 23–25, 27–28, 31,36, 40, 44
Iron, 20, 26–29

J

Jewelry, 7–8, 11–12, 29

K

Kazakhstan, 16
Klondike River, 9

L

Liberia, 12

M

Manufacturing, 8–9, 12, 17, 20, 27
Medicine, 32, 36
Metal, 6–9, 24, 26–28, 44
Middle East, 25, 29
Mineral, 31–33, 39–40
Mining, 8–9, 12–13, 19–21, 24, 27–28, 32, 38, 40
Money, 7–8, 11, 13, 32

N

Natural gas, 14–17, 24, 44
Natural Resources Canada, 32
New Zealand, 8, 37
Nonrenewable, 4, 7, 11, 15–16, 19, 23, 27, 31, 37, 39

O

Oil, 15, 22–25, 44
Ore, 8, 20, 28–29

P

Parkin, Timothy B., 40
Petroleum, 15–16, 24, 32
Plant, 9, 15, 19, 35, 39–40, 46
Politics, 24–25

R

Raw material, 15, 23–24, 28, 31, 44, 46
Renewable, 4, 35, 37, 43–44
Ross, Michael, 12
Russia, 12, 16

S

Salt, 23, 30–33
Settlement, 8–9, 32, 40, 46
Shelter, 35, 39
Sierra Leone, 12–13
Skagway, 9
Soil, 12, 16, 20, 35–41
South Africa, 8, 12, 29
South America, 8
Steel, 20, 27–29
Survival, 4, 31, 37, 40, 44, 46
Sustainable, 37, 43
Sweden, 29

T

Trade, 13, 28, 32–33
Transportation, 9, 24, 27–29, 32, 36
Trees, 34–37, 41

U

United States, 4, 8, 14–15, 29, 41
Uranium, 47

W

War, 7, 11, 13, 24–25
Well, 16–17, 23, 44
West, Larry, 44
Williams, Sam, 16

Y

Yukon, 9